ARMORED AND DANGEROUS

by Howard Zimmerman

Consultant: Luis M. Chiappe, Ph.D.
Director of the Dinosaur Institute
Natural History Museum of Los Angeles County

BEARPORT PUBLISHING

NEW YORK, NEW YORK

Credits

Title Page, © Luis Rey; TOC, © De Agostini Picture Library/Getty Images; 4-5, © John Bindon; 6, © De Agostini Picture Library/The Natural History Museum, London; 7, © Luis Rey; 8, © Luis Rey; 9, © Adam Stuart Smith; 10T, © Luis Rey; 10B, © Colin Keates/Dorling Kindersly; 11, © Phil Wilson; 12L, Courtesy of the Royal Tyrrell Museum, Drumheller, Alberta; 12R, © De Agostini Picture Library/Getty Images; 13, © Phil Wilson; 14-15, © Phil Wilson; 16-17, © De Agostini Picture Library/The Natural History Museum, London; 18T, © 2007 by Karen Carr and Karen Carr Studio; 18B, © photomandan/istockphoto; 19, © Luis Rey; 20, © De Agostini Picture Library/The Natural History Museum, London; 21, © John Bindon; 23TL, © Phil Wilson; 23TR, © Luis Rey; 23BL, © Vladimir Sazonov/Shutterstock; 23BR, © Luis Rey.

Publisher: Kenn Goin
Editorial Director: Adam Siegel
Creative Director: Spencer Brinker
Design: Dawn Beard Creative
Cover Illustration: Luis Rey
Photo Researcher: Omni-Photo Communications, Inc.

Library of Congress Cataloging-in-Publication Data

Zimmerman, Howard.
 Armored and dangerous / by Howard Zimmerman.
    p. cm. — (Dino times trivia)
 Includes bibliographical references and index.
 ISBN-13: 978-1-59716-712-3 (library binding)
 ISBN-10: 1-59716-712-6 (library binding)
 1. Ornithischia—Juvenile literature. 2. Dinosaurs—Juvenile literature. I. Title.

 QE862.O65Z56 2009
 567.915—dc22
                        2008006171

For more information, write to Bearport Publishing Company, Inc., 101 Fifth Avenue, Suite 6R, New York, New York 10003. Printed in the United States of America.

10 9 8 7 6 5 4 3 2

Contents

Dinosaur Tanks

Many meat-eating **dinosaurs** roamed the earth more than 65 million years ago. They used their sharp claws and teeth to hunt and kill.

How did other dinosaurs stay safe from them? Some were small and hid. Others ran away. Still others were too huge to hunt.

Many dinosaurs, however, were not small or fast or huge. How did they stay safe? Their bodies were covered in armor—like a tank.

In this book you'll meet eight armored dinosaurs. They couldn't outrun a meat-eater, but most knew how to fight back.

All armored
dinosaurs ate plants
instead of meat.

Scutellosaurus

How do you say it?
skoo-*tel*-oh-SOR-uhss

What does it mean?
small-shield reptile

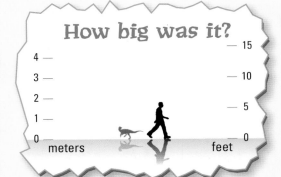

How big was it?

meters   feet

Scutellosaurus was one of the first armored dinosaurs. It had tough bony plates, called **scutes**, under its skin.

How did the scutes stop a hungry enemy from killing *Scutellosaurus*?

The scutes formed a kind of armor along the dinosaur's back, sides, and tail. They were so hard that some meat-eaters probably broke their teeth when they tried to bite through them.

Scutellosaurus

scutes

Unlike most other armored dinosaurs, *Scutellosaurus* was small and light enough to run on two legs instead of four.

Scelidosaurus

How do you say it?
skel-*ih*-doh-SOR-uhss

What does it mean?
limb reptile

How big was it?

meters	feet
4	15
3	10
2	5
1	
0	0

The scutes on *Scelidosaurus* were much bigger than those on *Scutellosaurus*.

How did these heavy scutes affect the way *Scelidosaurus* moved?

The dinosaur's armor weighed so much that *Scelidosaurus* couldn't stand up and run on two legs. The heavy scutes forced the animal to move on four legs instead.

scutes

Scelidosaurus and most other armored dinosaurs moved slowly because of their large, heavy plates.

9

Stegosaurus

How do you say it?
steg-oh-SOR-uhss

What does it mean?
covered reptile

How big was it?

4 — / 3 — / 2 — / 1 — / 0

— 15 / — 10 / — 5 / — 0

meters   feet

Stegosaurus had 17 large bony plates sticking up on the back of its body. These plates were too thin to keep *Stegosaurus* safe from a hungry enemy, however.

What did the animal use for protection instead?

Stegosaurus had four sharp spikes on its tail that it could swing from side to side. They could easily cut the skin of an attacker.

fossil of *Stegosaurus* tail spike

10

bony plates

spikes

At first, the scientist who discovered the **fossils** of *Stegosaurus* didn't know they were from a dinosaur. He thought he had found the bones of a giant turtle.

Ankylosaurus

How do you say it?
an-*kee*-loh-SOR-uhss

What does it mean?
stiff or fused reptile

How big was it?

Ankylosaurus was a very slow dinosaur.

Since it couldn't run away, how did it protect itself from speedy meat-eaters?

Ankylosaurus had a tail that ended in a huge **club** made of bone. It could use its tail to whack and break the leg of a dinosaur that got too close.

tail club

fossil of *Ankylosaurus* tail club

tail club

Ankylosaurus had armor made up of hundreds of bony plates in its skin. It even had small bony plates on its eyelids to protect its eyes.

13

Sauropelta

How do you say it?
saw-roh-PEL-tuh

What does it mean?
reptile shield

How big was it?

(scale: meters 0–4, feet 0–15)

Sauropelta had bony plates that ran from the back of its head down to the tip of its tail.

One part of this tank-like animal, however, wasn't protected with a layer of armor. What was it?

Sauropelta's belly had no bony plates to protect it.

If an enemy was able to flip *Sauropelta* over, it could easily sink its teeth and claws into the animal's stomach.

Hylaeosaurus

How big was it?

Hylaeosaurus didn't have a tail it could use as a club.

What weapons did it have instead?

Hylaeosaurus had sharp spikes sticking out along its sides and tail. The sharp spikes made it hard for a meat-eater to try and flip the animal over.

Edmontonia

What does it mean?
from Edmonton
(the rock formation in Alberta, Canada, where the first fossils were found)

How big was it?

Edmontonia was one of the biggest armored dinosaurs. It weighed around 6,000 pounds (2,722 kg)—about as much as a rhinoceros.

Like other armored dinosaurs, *Edmontonia* moved very slowly. How do scientists know?

Scientists have found footprints of armored dinosaurs that are spaced close together. The spacing shows that the fastest these animals could move was probably about six miles per hour (10 kph).

rhinoceros

Scientists can tell how fast an animal moves by looking at its footprints. When an animal moves quickly, the footprints are spaced far apart. When it moves slowly, they are close together.

Talarurus

How big was it?

The head and body of an adult *Talarurus* were covered in armor. The dinosaur even had a layer of bone on top of its skull.

How was a baby *Talarurus* different from an adult?

A baby didn't have armor to protect its head.

20

Some armored dinosaurs, such as *Pinacosaurus* (pih-nak-oh-SOR-uhss), lived together when they were babies. Scientists have found several of their fossils buried together.

baby *Pinacosaurus*

21

Where Did They Live?

This map shows some of the places where the fossils of armored dinosaurs have been found.

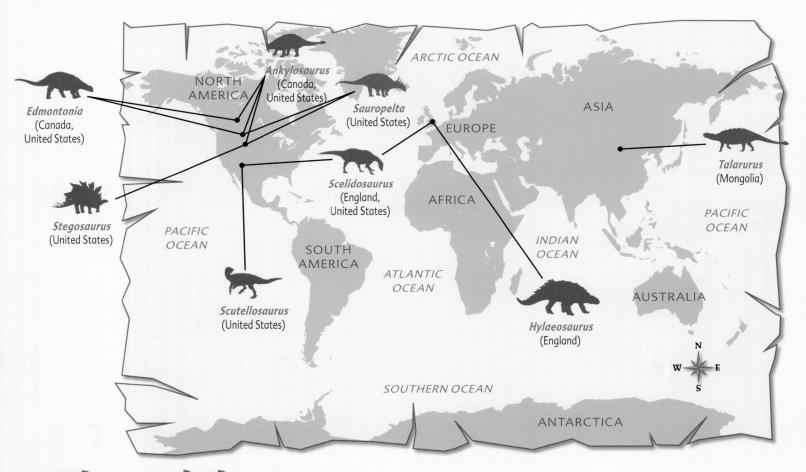

Edmontonia
(Canada, United States)

Stegosaurus
(United States)

ARCTIC OCEAN

NORTH AMERICA

Ankylosaurus
(Canada, United States)

Sauropelta
(United States)

EUROPE

ASIA

Talarurus
(Mongolia)

PACIFIC OCEAN

Scelidosaurus
(England, United States)

AFRICA

PACIFIC OCEAN

SOUTH AMERICA

ATLANTIC OCEAN

INDIAN OCEAN

Scutellosaurus
(United States)

AUSTRALIA

Hylaeosaurus
(England)

N
W E
S

SOUTHERN OCEAN

ANTARCTICA

When Did They Live?

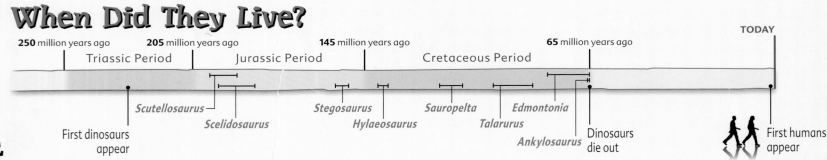

TODAY

250 million years ago   205 million years ago   145 million years ago   65 million years ago

Triassic Period   Jurassic Period   Cretaceous Period

Scutellosaurus

Scelidosaurus

Stegosaurus

Hylaeosaurus

Sauropelta

Talarurus

Edmontonia

Ankylosaurus

First dinosaurs appear

Dinosaurs die out

First humans appear

Glossary

club (KLUHB) the part of a dinosaur's tail that was used like a big stick to hit an enemy

dinosaurs (DYE-nuh-sorz) reptiles that lived on land more than 65 million years ago, and then died out

fossils (FOSS-uhlz) what is left of plants or animals that lived long ago

scutes (SKYOOTS) bony plates just under or on top of the skin that protected a dinosaur's neck, back, or tail

Index

Read More

Hughes, Monica. *Fighting Dinosaurs.* New York: Bearport Publishing (2008).

Lessem, Don. *Armored Dinosaurs.* Minneapolis, MN: Lerner Publications (2005).

Learn More Online

To learn more about armored dinosaurs, visit
www.bearportpublishing.com/DinoTimesTrivia

About the Author

Howard Zimmerman is the author of two books on prehistoric animals. He has also created and edited several picture books that dramatize the lives of prehistoric creatures.